Prodigal
from the
Parsonage

by Deanna Neely

Published by
Advance Ministries • Willis, TX

Prodigal from the Parsonage

by Deanna Neely

Copyright © 2001 by Advance Ministries
Willis, TX 77318
www.advanceministries.org
All rights reserved.

ISBN: 0-9706034-2-8

Printed in the United States of America by
Morris Publishing • 3212 East Highway 30
Kearney, NE 68847 • 1-800-650-7888

Table of Contents

Preface	1
Three Wills	5
Blasphemy	9
Garbage In...	15
Parenting in the Parsonage	17
School Daze	23
Privacy in the Parsonage	29
The Gumball Ring	31
Burnout	33
Mama Cares	37
Preachers Are Human, Too	41
Since I'm Going to Hell Anyway	45
The Lost Sheep	49
There's No Place Like Home	59
Of Love and Relationships	63
Views From the Pews	69
Jesus, Not Denise, Died for Me!	73
Encounter With God's Love	79
The Parent's Perspective	85
A Brother's Viewpoint	99

Preface

A certain man had two sons. One day the youngest came and said to his Father, "Father, give me the share of the property that is coming to me." So the father apportioned to both of them their inheritance.

After a few days the younger son collected all he had and traveled to a distant country, and there he squandered what he had in reckless living. When he had run through everything, a terrible famine visited that whole land and he began to lack; so he went and hired himself out to a citizen of that country, who sent him into his fields to tend hogs.

He longed to have his stomach filled with bean pods, which the hogs were eating, but no one gave him any. But when he came to himself, he said, "How many of my father's hired hands have more than they can eat, and here I am starving. I will get up and go to my father and say to him, 'Father, I have sinned against heaven and before you, and I no longer deserve to be called your son. Take me on as one of your hired hands.'"

So he got up and went to his father; but when he was still a great distance away, his father saw him and felt deeply moved and, running, fell on his neck and kissed him. The son said to him, "Father, I have sinned against heaven and before you; I no longer deserve to be called your son." But the father told the servants, "Hurry! Fetch the choicest robe and put it on him, put a ring on his hand and sandals on his feet; bring the fatted calf, too, and butcher it. Let us feast and be merry, for this my son was dead and he has come to life again; he was lost and has been found." (This inspiring story was taken from Luke 15:11-32.)

Don't you just love stories with happy endings? Your own prodigal from the parsonage can be a story with a happy ending.

My mother and I were talking last Friday

and I was asking her about different preachers' children in their fellowship. As I said the preachers' names, she would answer with the number of children in their family, how many were prodigals, and their ages. I was surprised to learn there are a lot of prodigals between the ages of 20 and 45.

Mother spoke to a Womens' Conference in Texas about *The Prodigal From The Parsonage*, since she had first-hand knowledge by having me. We discussed the feelings a preacher and his wife have when their own child walks away from God.

We hope this book that God and Mama inspired me to write will help you understand the perspective of the prodigals from the parsonage. Perhaps some light will be shed on how to better understand your prodigal by sharing what happened with us.

1

Three Wills

The question I'm asked most when people learn I was a backslidden preacher's kid is, "What made you backslide?" And just like anyone else, I answer, "I'm not sure. It didn't happen overnight."

Preacher's children are especially blessed. It should be an honor for us to have been born to parents dedicated to God's service. And the privilege to have their prayers to follow us. Some of us, however, are slow learners, not realizing how great a role we can play for our heavenly Father.

As preachers' children we become so accustomed to hearing prayers and scriptures quoted until the reason we're on this earth slides into the background. To think, I had special training on how to deal with different situations—from smiling when I had to smile to simple etiquette. After all the additional opportunities preachers' children are given, God left us the most wonderful gift...the power of choice!

I was taught there are three wills in a person's life:

1. God's will
2. The devil's will
3. Man's will

I'll confess—my backsliding was the result of my personal choices. I chose my own will. I had finally come to grips with this dishonesty that had been building inside of me for years. It seemed to be growing. I knew every time I sang or played a special part, it wasn't from my heart.

I decided, "If I'm going to hell for lying, it won't be for lying to myself, sitting here on the pew, pretending I'm ready for heaven."

Why am I living this way? For Daddy? So I won't ruin his ministry? It bothered me that I had let religion become a way of life. Being raised in a very sheltered environment, I knew nothing about the world and the farther I slipped away from God, the more curious I became of the things of the world. You can only pretend so long and you either pray through to a new experience with Jesus Christ, or give Him up and go all out for the devil.

The Bible states in Matthew 6:24, and again in Luke 16:13: "No man can serve two masters: for either he will hate the one, and love the other; or else he will hold to the one and despise the other. Ye cannot serve God and mammon."

The last time I prayed, I said, "God, I don't want to live this way right now. If I'm ever anything, I will be Pentecostal, and I realize it's serious to play with You, so until I get right, I won't ask you for anything."

And I didn't!

2

Blasphemy!

It isn't wise to compare your children—especially their walk with God. Remember, one child may not grasp spiritual concerns as quickly as another. Some of us are slow learners.

I had a twin sister who ran circles around me. She took after Daddy, and I paced slower, like Mama. She was aggressive and I was bashful. She was a leader and did most of the talking. Denise learned early what it took to live for God, accepted it as a way of life and was happy living for God.

On the other hand, I was not that self-assured, was easily intimidated, was swayed by peer pressure, and at times ashamed of being stamped a Pentecostal preacher's kid.

Let's go back to when I was eight years old. During church I sometimes liked to sit beside Sue. She was a growny girl in high school and would let me look at her pictures. This was the era of seeing how many pictures you could fit into a fold-over billfold without breaking the snap. Looking carefully at each picture twice could usually take the entire sermon.

At other times Denise and I would sit on the front row with Bibles and pens, writing down every scripture the preacher used.

On July 30, 1963, we were on the front row. Denise had been praying regularly for the Holy Ghost and had already gotten baptized a year earlier, but I had not followed suit. On this day, we both went to the altar and received the Holy Ghost. From then on, Denise had a daily walk with God. She didn't care who, when, how or what was happening. She was always proud to be Pentecostal.

It wasn't too long until I started doubting that I had received the Holy Ghost. (A child's trials are as big to them as trials are to adults and parents.) I got out my Bible and read where I had written in the front of it, like kids do:

Deanna Jane Neely
P.O. Box 3653
Odessa, Texas

FE2-6479 or FE2-8931 (call first)
August 7, 1954 (When I was born)

Received Holy Ghost- July 30, 1963. Baptized August 4, 1963. In Bro. Gilmore's revival. Spoke in another language. I was 8 years old when received Holy Ghost and was baptized.

Below this crude writing in green ink in the back of my Bible I wrote:

I really didn't get the Holy Ghost, I played like I spoke in tongues.
By Deanna Neely

I thought no more about it until Mama and

Daddy came and sat me down and Daddy asked, "Deanna, what is this you wrote in the back of your Bible?" One good rule in our house was: Don't write anything you couldn't say out loud. I just ducked my head and shrugged my shoulders.

"Well, Deanna," Daddy asked real calmly (but I sensed a storm inside), "Do you mean you and Denise shouted and spoke in tongues for over an hour and you're saying now you were just playing?" I started crying. He began to say, "Honey, did you know that it is a sin to deny the Holy Ghost. That's blasphemy! And blasphemy is the only sin God won't ever forgive."

He opened my Bible to Mark 3:29 and read to me: "But he that shall blaspheme against the Holy Ghost hath never forgiveness, but is in danger of eternal damnation."

Instead of closing my Bible then, he turned back to where I had written this unpardonable sin. I felt so ashamed, and wanted him so badly to close my Bible. "That means I can't ever go to heaven?" I said between sobs. "No," Daddy said, "I really don't believe you wrote this meaning to blaspheme. The devil would love to make you doubt you spoke in tongues. But God sees your heart and He'll forgive you, but be careful to never deny the Holy Ghost. You can backslide and say I don't have the Holy Ghost now, but it's dangerous when you say there's nothing to the Holy Ghost."

Proverbs 22:6: "Train up a child in the way he should go, and when he is old, he will not depart from it."

That memorable incident never left me during my prodigal years. I would have told anyone, "I was raised Pentecostal, but now I'm nothing." (How true, without God, I really was nothing.)

3

Garbage in...

During the summers, while growing up, my sister and I would go to our Pappaw and Big Mama Van Winkles'. We could not have been any enjoyment to them, for the entire time we stayed with them, we lay lifeless in front of a television. Even to the point of watching all the commercials.

After a week of staying with our grandparents, we would come home two different girls. We were talking, walking, and trying to play like we were movie stars. If one week had that effect on us, what would a lifetime do?

It must have been Mother and Daddy's

prayers, because to this day I don't—and never did—care for TV that much. I dreamt so bad until it wasn't worth filling my head with all those worldly lusts.

How easily we can lose the individualism that God has placed in each one of us to be different.

Last year, the teenage suicide rates were higher than ever in history. I can understand why! No one can live up to the false and plastic world that comes across the movie screen. We are what we think, and the Bible says to "think on pure things." You can't read Rosemary Rogers books and think pure thoughts.

4

Parenting in the Parsonage

During the most impressionable years of a child, it is so important for parents to teach and be an example of the adult you want your children to become.

The first commandment instructs us to "love the Lord thy God with all thy heart, and with all thy soul, and with all thy might." The next instructions He gave us in Deuteronomy 6:7: "And thou shalt teach them diligently unto thy children, and shalt talk of them when thou sittest in thine house, and when thou walkest by the way, and when thou liest down, and when thou risest up." It is so important to "hide the word" in our hearts so we can keep sin out.

You parents may be asking yourselves, "Well, the children are raised. We thought at the time we were teaching them and being a living example of parents who loved the Lord with all their hearts—and now they are backslidden!?" DON'T TAKE IT PERSONAL! Your child being a prodigal does not necessarily reflect on the Christian you were in your home. Be consoled by the fact that if you did live a Christian life in front of your children, the Bible gives you hope and a promise: "Train up a child in the way he should go: and when he is old, he will not depart from it" (Proverbs 22:6). When they do come back home, and decide to live their lives for God, how diligently you taught them as a child will be seen by how strong their personal devotion is to God.

The saying, "You really don't know someone until you live with them," is so true. Of all people, your children have watched you and your walk with God their entire lives. No, they may have not seen each time you hid away in your closet and prayed, but your actions showed each time you did and each time you needed to.

During my years of growing up, I may not remember the exact words my parents used to discipline me, but I remember the actions that were used.

When giving a speech, one is taught three principal rules:

1. Tell them what you're going to tell them.
2. Tell them.
3. Tell them what you have told them.

I believe my dad must have used these three rules when it was our time to get a spanking. He never failed to set us on the side of the bed and explain to us why we were getting punished. (Of course, during this time we were praying and promising we wouldn't ever do it again!) After the spanking, he would set us on the side of the bed again and remind us that he loved us and make us hug his neck. Although I went through this routine more often than I care to admit, I can truthfully say that daddy's actions said more than his words.

DON'T COMPROMISE. Although it may seem easier to compromise, and you think you may be doing permanent damage by being so hard, think twice. You will be losing your child's respect for you if you let down your beliefs.

During my years as the prodigal, I always knew that my parents weren't going to change. They were the stronghold and if they had compromised with the world, it would not have been something I would have wanted to come home to.

People can be so disappointing! Don't disregard anything your kids tell you just because they're children. If they have the Holy Ghost, their spirit senses things and people to watch out for. Some saints tend to get on the level of the preachers' kids.

Remember when the giant hairdos were in? Well, my sister always could fix her hair so well, and back then, the bigger the better. Some dear saint in our church complained to Daddy. I might add that her hair seemed just as high, but Daddy asked Denise to make hers smaller, and she did. It was just a shame that this particular lady lowered herself to a child's level to get even with something preached over the pulpit!

Don't forget: the preacher and his wife have real children, just like the saints. Sometimes its reassuring to have your Mama defend you when you overhear accusations. Mamas, don't *always* defend your children, or you will begin to stick your head in the sand and fail to recognize the pitfalls your child is approaching.

My sister was one who didn't mind asking "why?" Me, I wanted to get any confrontation over with in a hurry, so I didn't say much, just kept it inside. On the outside, this may appear to be a model child. I can't remember the number of times I'd nudge Denise and whisper, "Hush! Quit asking why! You know it only makes it worse!" She always thought she had to know "why" to every instruction or answer my parents gave us. It never really bothered me one way or the other unless I really had my heart set on something. Even then I wouldn't speak up, but I would just write it in my mind's notebook: "If I ever get out of here...."

This only bred resentment against my parents. It would have been better to ask "why."

5

School Daze

I had my victories as a teenager growing up. I knew what it was like to experience God's blessings. No one could ever take that away from me. It is so important to pray for your children for the Holy Ghost—then allow the Holy Ghost to direct them. Give God a chance to help them make their own connections.

Here we are in junior high. All the girls are suiting out for gym class. The band is marching on the other end of the field, and our class has come out to run laps. The P.E. uniforms are green shorts and white shirts, but mother has so righteously made us culottes. It is worth it to me to run one lap and complain to the teacher I was having an asthma attack so I could sit it out or go in. I'm not sure...was that a lie—a sin just as bad as wearing indecent apparel? How embarrassing the whole scene was!

Winter came and tumbling became our fitness program. The P. E. teacher sent us home with a note to Mama:

> *Mrs. Neely,*
> *In regards to your daughters' PE uniforms, I really would like to advise you that they are more immodest in culottes than they would be in shorts.*

This was the first year we had gone to a junior high, and it was a most impressionable age. Resentment began to build. I didn't accept being different without me having a choice. But I wore the culottes and never questioned, but in my heart I knew that whenever I got old enough....

I wonder if Mama and Daddy had given us the choice (without trying to place any guilt), or given God a chance to talk to us, letting us choose between singing in the choir and participating in church activities, or wearing the P. E. uniform, would I have chosen the church and had a victory in my heart, having made my first conviction on my own?

If your children have the Holy Ghost, even at an early age, Jesus can speak to their hearts with convictions. When He does the work, the conviction is permanent in the child's heart.

Let me share with you a little about nerves. My first and only time of giving a speech was in the 10th grade. My sister Denise and I were in the same English class and it came book report day. Denise was first. While she was giving her report, I was making all sorts of faces trying to distract her. She stopped talking and very seriously said, "Mr. Cleghorn, would you please do something about her distracting me?"

So Mr. Cleghorn said, "Deanna, go stand in the hall until Denise is finished." When Denise had completed her report, Mr. Cleghorn called me into the room to give mine. I had read a book on the

Renassiance Period, so I readily got up in front of the class. "My book report today is on the Renassie Age." Denise started slapping her leg and fell out in the floor laughing—ha, ha, ha. Needless to say that ended both my book report and my speaking career.

I believe that one reason I did backslide during those years was because sports were important to me—racketball, water skiing, and baseball. It was that lust that drew me away, and the devil tries to make you think you are being cheated by missing out on these things. Just think how good you might have been if you could have played all during those earlier years!

If your children have the Holy Ghost, let them make a few connections on their own. Sitting out of the church activities may mean more than a P. E. uniform. After all, peer pressure is greatest in those early teen years. Popularity is a dead cinch when you are the kid in the parsonage, but not always, however, when you are attending a big school and don't quite fit in.

It's the little things that build to insurmountable imaginations in your mind as a young person. I say, keep your imagination under control!

I would like to suggest that parents pray that the Holy Ghost will direct their children, rather than them living for God through force or fear. Don't give up! What you've taught them all of their lives will always be with them.

6

Privacy in the Parsonage

My sister and I had just begun our sophomore year in high school when Daddy came in with the news, "We're moving!" I was excited because one of the boys I was corresponding with at the time was the pastor's son of a neighboring church in that area. How convenient!

My sister didn't take the news quite as well. I really thought the girl was going to have a nervous breakdown at age fifteen. After viewing the parsonage we'd be moving into, I was even more excited. I was going to get to have a bedroom all to myself—until I found out which bedroom it would be.

In the front part of the parsonage, there was a bedroom with red carpet and matching velvet drapes—so great for a fifteen-year-old. Of course, since my sister was taking the move so hard, she got this lovely red bedroom, which left me with a small, uncarpeted bedroom with five doors entering into it. The worst part was when visiting ministers came to the parsonage after church, Daddy would bring them through my room since one of the five doors was the back door to the carport.

7

The Gumball Ring

A special friend shared with me an incident that occurred in their parsonage. Her daughter placed a coin in a gum ball machine that also had prizes in clear eggs. Out came one of the clear eggs with a little toy ring.

Excitedly, she ran over to her mother and grandmother to show them her prize. As the young preacher's wife was about to take the ring away from the child, the grandmother pulled her aside and gave her a very wise bit of advice. "Let her play with it; she'll grow tired of it, but if you take it away now, and tell her we teach against jewelry, resentment might begin to form in her heart."

Sure enough, the small girl played with the ring and even wore it places. But just as the grandmother said, it was just a toy and was soon broken or lost. The wise words of the grandmother, with the cooperation of the mother, probably avoided resentment in the child's heart against her mother.

A parent has to be careful when imposing a personal conviction upon a child, even if it's as small as a toy.

8

Burnout

As a child I remember many an endless hour sitting at small municipal airports. Mother would be in the front seat busy with her needlework, and my brother Mike, Denise and I would be in the back seat talking very civil to one another.

We'd tell Mother, "Mama, we'll go check out the airplanes ourselves and let you know which one Daddy ought to buy!" and bail out of the car to go shopping. We'd then head back to the car with our results. All the while, Daddy was still bent over looking under or into some little plane.

After reporting our findings, we'd play games like "Red Light, Green Light" or "Mother,

May I." The wind would blow so hard until our lips and cheeks would look sunburned, they would be so chapped! We would wearily crawl into the back seat of the car moaning, "I wish he'd hurry up and come on." Then Daddy would head toward the car and we would all get excited. "Hurry, move over, here comes Daddy." Invariably, a salesman or an owner would walk out from an airplane hanger and intercept him. It didn't take long to learn that this meant another hour of waiting. For nothing! Mother always seemed so calm, for she had been through this wait quite a few times before.

By the time I reached twelve years of age, I didn't care if I ever saw another airport except to go get in the airplane to go somewhere. It was one of Daddy's loves, but to me it was a definite BURNOUT!

Children raised in and around the church can begin to think like I did at the airport.

After a few Bible lessons were learned, and I began to get older, I started to tire of hearing the same stories. My choices were either going into the young people's class or teach the same stories to the younger children. I chose teaching the younger group. I got involved with children's church and the bus ministry. Looking back, I realize it was an escape from having to go to the church service on Sunday morning.

At sixteen, I needed to be learning why I believed the children's song I had sung, "One, One, One, One way to God," rather than teaching the same stories over and over. I found myself not maturing as a Christian because I wasn't in a place to grow. I was remaining on the level of a small child rather than growing spiritually. In smaller churches the need for Sunday school teachers is often so great that the pastor's children teach the younger kids. This may help out when there's a shortage of teachers, but young teenagers need to learn rather then teach.

By age seventeen, I had no interest in learning anything else in the Bible. I had sat and listened to Daddy tell numbers of people about "one God," how to receive the Holy Ghost, and could recite it to you, but it never penetrated my heart.

9

Mama Cares

Don't take it for granted that your children know how to pray through a trial just because they've been raised in a preacher's home (even when they are young adults).

I remember my first love. He was tall and handsome. His hair was strawberry blond complimented by brown eyes and eyelashes batting his eyebrows. He and another young preacher attending Bible college came to our house for one of their first revivals. I thought he did so good when he preached. I loved him so much I even took piano lessons because I knew preachers wives needed to play the quiet organ behind their husband's altar calls.

My Daddy was aware that his daughter had finally given her heart to this man and drove me sixty miles, one way, to hear him preach at a nearby town in West Texas. We were both young, and so smitten with each other until we wrote every day.

On this particular day, I came home from school, and sure enough, there was a letter lying on the desk. One good thing that was taught in our home was never to open any mail unless it was addressed to you.

So I hurriedly ripped open the envelope, my heart fluttering, only to read:

Dear Deanna,

I've been praying about our future together and I really feel that I'm going to be preaching a lot of different places, so let's just cool it for awhile and maybe someday....

My heart was broken. I went crying into the kitchen and sat at the bar while Mama was cooking dinner and asked her to read my letter. Mama read the letter and looked at me as I used the kitchen towel to blow my nose, and said, "Deanna, you just need to go pray through."

This was not a new term in our house, but at this moment I wanted Mama to sympathize with me. I headed off down the hall to my bedroom, but something happened between the kitchen and my closet—I rebelled.

I stomped back into the kitchen and put my hands on my hips and said, "Well, Mama, if he doesn't like me and he thinks I'm not good enough for him, he can just go find someone else. I don't need him!"

It's a different thing today when Mama tells me to go pray through. She always says, "Deanna, you go to your closet, and I'll go to mine." There is strength in knowing that my Mama cares enough about me to stop what she is doing, and pray with me.

10

Preachers Are Human, Too

Oftentimes children allow very little room for parents to err. When you're the parent and the preacher too, people tend to put you in a glass house and then test you to see how much pressure you can stand up under.

One of the first stories I heard as a child was taken from II Kings 2:23,24. It became a favorite. I visualize Elisha as a big man, shoulders slightly humped, kind of ugly, and he was going down a dusty road to Bethel. Little children were playing along the side of the road and dared each other to say something to the man. So the dare-devils of the group began to mock Elisha chanting, "Go up, old Baldy! Go up, old Baldy!"

It must have hit Elisha wrong because He stopped, turned around and cursed them in the name of the Lord. Lo, here came two big mama bears out of the woods and ripped up forty-two of those little mockers.

Needless to say, as a child hearing this story, the lesson to not make fun of anyone and reverence the ministry was imbedded deep in my heart! But as I re-read the story later in life, I realized how human Elisha was. That seemed to be harsh punishment for forty-two kids making sport of an old man.

Mothers play an important role in making the children understand that their Dad is a "Man of God" and a regular Daddy also. There is a difference between reverence for your Dad as a "Man of God," and being scared to death to cross him.

I was fourteen years old when I saw that my Dad was really a "Man of God." It was the first year our church had organized a Bible quiz team and we had First and Second Corinthians practically memorized. It was Sunday afternoon, the day of the final challenge quiz in our section. It was held at a church across town. On the way to the quiz, I told Daddy, "I don't think I want to be in it." Wow! Did I ever say the wrong words!

Daddy was quite angry and after a hard shaking and talking to, I did sit at the quiz table but my heart was not in it. It would've been just as well for me not to have been there.

Later in the evening service at our church, song service had just finished and the choir was filing back to their seats. As I was coming down from the choir loft, my Daddy met me in the middle of the aisle. He hugged me and whispered, "Deanna, I wasn't right in how I treated you today at the Bible quiz. Will you forgive me?" I must say, I was quite shocked. Daddy was asking me to forgive him?

"Yeah!" I muttered with tears coming to my eyes. I sat and listened intently in church that night as my Dad had just become a "Man of God" in my eyes—and yet I knew he was human.

11

Since I'm Going to Hell Anyway....

The hardest time for me to come home was the first time after deciding, "If I'm going to hell anyway, lying while I am sitting here on the pew, it won't be for lying to myself."

So I completely backslid to the point that everyone else could see it up front. Then came time to go home. Mama and Daddy just kept staring and treated me like a stranger. I finally went in the kitchen at the parsonage and tried to talk to Mama. It was like she hardly knew me. Sooooo polite. I walked over to the stove where she was cooking and took her face in my hands and said,

"Mama, I'm still Deanna, your daughter. Please don't treat me like a visitor. I may look different on the outside but I am still the same on the inside. I've just decided to be honest to God and myself." Tears began to roll down her cheeks as she hugged me and whispered, "Oh, I never thought that one of ya'll would backslide."

Both the prodigal and the parents have a lot of mixed feelings after the first reunion of openly admitting, "I don't want to live for God right now."

In James 1:14, it reads: "But every man is tempted, when he is drawn away of his own lust, and enticed." When you start slipping and giving in to fleshly desires, the devil puts it into your mind that you might as well give up entirely.

It's not what you as parents have done to cause your children to backslide. The lust of fleshly desires became stronger than our spirit. Today, I understand that without a daily walk with God, you cannot live in the world without becoming weaker and weaker. A new friend, an old grandma who really loves the Lord, reminds me often: "The devil is mighty, but God is Almighty." We must daily submit our lives and bodies to the will of God or we will be tempted and drawn away by our own lusts.

12

The Lost Sheep

A lost sheep chooses another god to replace the one true God. Their god could become drugs, drinking, smoking, sports, movies/televisions, men's apparel, cut hair, or adultery/fornication.

By worshiping the creature rather than Creator, you do everything the creature desires...even the bizarre. Any number of things can be made gods. Usually a person chooses more than just one god. At times you may not understand where your prodigal is coming from because their god is the #1 priority at this time in their life. It's not that they love you any less, but let's face it—they are not comfortable being around you like in past days. Conviction and other gods keep them away.

Don't be alarmed when they aren't as cooperative with family gatherings—the devil has conveniently given them another family. They still love you just as much, and probably talk admiringly when telling others about you. After awhile, this new foreign family who, like in the prodigal son's story, helped him blow his money, will deceive the backslider. This adds to the bitterness in their heart against people.

The defense—"If I don't take care of myself, no one else will"—becomes the motto. After being raised sheltered, it doesn't take long to become calloused to keep from being so easily hurt the next time. Before long, one becomes selfish and self-centered in order to survive in the cruel world.

I thought, "Too many years I went home on all holidays, etc., just because Mama and Daddy wanted me to. But now I'm going to do all the things I never got to do in the parsonage!" Since a preacher's workdays are the prodigal's days off, you go weeks, months, and sometimes years without seeing them.

We all know the story of the lost sheep in the Bible, how the shepherd so gently and patiently went out to search for him and carried him back to the flock. I want to tell you about another lost sheep in the Bible. He has always kind of been my hero. I never realized my life would be patterned after his.

After a certain man and his wife learned they were going to bear a son, they inquired of the angel of the Lord, "How shall we raise this son? What shall be the lad's way of life and his activities?" The angel told them no razor should ever touch his head. His mother must not partake of wine or strong drink or any unclean food, for he shall be a Nazarite from the time of conception until his death.

The time came and she bore a son and called his name Samson. The child grew up and the Lord blessed him. When Samson was of marriageable age, he told his parents about a woman he wanted for his wife. On his way to Timnah to visit her, he passed by a vineyard and a lion came roaring out against him. This was the first time the Bible tells us that the spirit of the Lord came upon him, and he fought the lion and tore him apart with his bare hands.

When he came back later to marry the Timnahite, he passed that place and there was the carcass of the lion filled with honey. Sweet victory! He shared the honey with his parents, but didn't tell them where he got it.

Now the time came for seven days of fasting and Samson's first lesson of how people can disappoint you. He had challenged thirty men of Timnah with a riddle. They pressured his new wife to entice him to reveal its meaning. He finally became so weary from her nagging until he finally broke and told her the meaning of the riddle, and she used it against him. The Spirit of the Lord came upon him again and he killed thirty men for their clothes and paid his debt—only to find they had given his wife to his best man while he had been away. Another disappointment in people.

But the Lord came upon Samson again and he went and caught 300 foxes, tied them together tail to tail. Then he made torches and put one between each pair of tails. He set fire to the torches and turned the foxes loose in the grain fields of the Philistines, so that the shocks, standing grain, and olive groves were burned. After the Philistines learned that it was Samson who had done the damage, they burned his wife and her father.

When Samson learned what they had done, he slaughtered many Philistines and then went to hide in the rocks. Three thousand men from Judah came to the rock where Samson was hiding and told Samson, "You're making life hard for us, so we're going to openly turn you over to the Philistines. We will not kill you but we are going to bind you securely and deliver you into their hands." They bound him with new ropes and brought him away from the rock.

When the Philistines shouted against him, the Spirit of the Lord came rushing upon him and ropes around his arms became as flax that had been burned with fire; they dropped from his hands. He found a jawbone of a donkey, and taking it in his hand, he killed a thousand men.

Now Samson must've started getting a little cocky with his special blessing, assured that he had special strength. He went down to Gaza and visited a prostitute. The Gazites discovered he was there and plotted to kill him but he got up at midnight and left—with the doors of the city gate on his shoulder! Later he fell in love with a woman by the name of Delilah.

He started being tempted unnecessarily, and began to play with the enemy, boasting of his strength, not knowing the enemy was ploying for his soul. Delilah used her seductive powers and after three times, Samson was beginning to weaken. She questioned his love, and then began nagging until his soul was wearied to death, and he opened his heart to her.

After coaxing him to lay his head on her lap, she cut off his hair and his strength left. Then Delilah exclaimed, "The Philistines are upon you,

Samson!" He awoke, shook himself, only to find that the Lord had departed from him. The Philistines seized him, put out his eyes and bound him in chains and put him to grinding in the prison. I imagine he had a lot of time to think while he was grinding, and his hair began to grow. He remembered his raising and all the mighty things he had done.

The time came for Samson to entertain the Philistines. A boy led him to the Coliseum, and Samson asked the boy to let him feel the supporting pillars of the building. The boy led him over to the pillars and Samson prayed one last prayer, "O Lord God, remember me, I pray thee, and strengthen me, I pray thee, only this once, O God, that I may be at once avenged of the Philistines for my two eyes." And with all his might, he flexed those muscles that had been so long unflexed, and the building caved in, killing him and many of the Philistines.

As parents you prayed for guidance and instruction from God on how to raise your children. The children grew and they were blessed. At the early age of 8, I received the Holy Ghost. Like Samson, as long as he had his hair, the Lord never left him; as long as we were faithful to God, He never left us.

All the years I was backslidden, I never wavered from the truth. I was a disobedient child. God knew where I was all the time. Children can become cocky with their inside line to the ministry. They take the blessings of God for granted. I became curious with the world. I had been taught the right way, but like Samson, I played with the enemy too long. When I finally got up to shake myself, God had left me, the devil had gotten me to forget that God could forgive me and I, like Samson, opened my heart to Delilah.

For a season, I thought, "This is great," but soon the plastic, superficial exterior wore thin. After the devil knew he had me chained, he put me to grinding. Did you know the devil will turn on you after he gets you? The lights and action look so enticing, but after he's got you, he'll wear you out and let you destroy your own temple. But while I was grinding, I remembered and wondered where God was.

You can never get totally away from what was put into your heart as a child.

13

There's No Place Like Home
(especially when you're sick)

Of all the days to be sick, it had to be today! The big boss is to be in town from Michigan and here I am at home, ill with the 24-hour virus.

Lying in bed, I began thinking about when I was a child, staying home from school sick, listening to all the family noises. Usually, when I heard my brother and sister come in from school, I got healed instantly. But to want to stay home at our house, you had to really be sick because house rules were: If you're sick enough to stay home, you're too sick to get out of bed. If you really weren't sick that morning, it would make you sick—sick of bed! By the time the next dawn cracked, I was ready and eager to go to school.

Reminiscing, I heard the telephone ringing and Mama's soft voice talking with someone on the phone...Mama running through my bedroom to check on how I was feeling with a cold wet rag and a 7-Up...the constant sounds of the washer plugging away on the clothes and the dryer whirling. It all created quite a picture.

I stopped day-dreaming long enough to get up and find a few towels to wash and placed them in the washing machine and started it up. As soon as I laid down and thought, "Now this really sounds like home," I feel asleep.

We did get special treatment when we stayed home. Sometimes Daddy would come through and lay his hand on my forehead and pray. He always smiled and finished with, "I believe you'll be all right."

I remember how good he smelled.

My dreams of childhood days were suddenly disturbed as the piercing ring of the telephone woke me with a jolt. No one knows I'm home from work, I thought, as I reached for the receiver. "Hello," I answered with a question in my voice.

The same sweet voice that I had just been reminiscing about came over the phone. "Are you all right?" "Mama!" I exclaimed shockingly, "How did you know I was at home? Did you call work?" "No," she answered, "I was just making my bed and something said, 'Deanna's at home sick today,' so I called to check on you."

After our conversation, I thanked God for such a Mama. Some could claim it was a mother's intuition, but I want to think that just like all those years I didn't serve God, I believe she still had this special gift to stop and pray for me—even when I wanted no part of it. How fortunate I am to have been born to such a Mama.

Well, mother's intuition or not, I felt special that out of the clear she knew.

14

Of Love And Relationships

"God, I don't like being single," I moaned silently, as I observed the couples meandering by. It was the first day of Spring and so beautiful until I decided to go to the park during lunch break. I picked the perfect park bench. The lake was lapping against the bank and ever so often the sun would reflect a unique sparkle in the waves. The birds were chirping so happily, but my heart wasn't happy.

This was my first Spring being a single Pentecostal young person. My heart ached for a special man in my life to share the wakening of the season. As I watched the different couples, I noticed there were those who looked at one another with admiration and love. Then I spotted a middle-aged man whose hair was gray around the temples and thinning on top. He had a few more wrinkles than most. My gazing turned into a stare as the older gentleman intrigued me. He appeared to be quite alone—lost in his own world. Yet somehow it seemed that he was content with his lot, that love was not lacking in his life as it was in mine.

Alone...but loved.

Although for a moment it seemed that there was a strange connection with this man, he never appeared to notice me and we went our separate ways without speaking. Perhaps the link was mutual loneliness...or was this an angel who was sent to me with a subtle message that even though I was alone I was still loved? I will never know for sure, but the message got through to me.

We were not made to be alone. That was not God's original plan. We are ever in search of a fulfilling relationship. While there's nothing wrong with that, it is in our relationships where the greatest spiritual danger lies. How easily we can be led. How quickly we can discover our vulnerability—often after it is too late.

I have come to see myself in that light—vulnerable. Making poor choices had become a bad habit, and one hard to break. As I look back, I can see how different things could have been if I had not kept company with those who really didn't care about God or my soul. I think Mama read me a scripture once about bad company corrupting good manners.

I remember that funny Bible verse where Solomon said, "It is better to dwell in a corner of the housetop, than with a brawling woman in a wide house." We used to laugh when they quoted that verse, but I think I know now what he was talking about. I guess there are some things worse than living alone.

But when you have no close companion, and not close to God or family...it is the pits.

I have compiled some thoughts and meditations that have come to my mind along the way:

Gain something from each relationship you enter.

Pentecostal dating is so different from what is practiced in the world.

Peer pressure is awesome...if you date steadily, peers have you nearly married.

Choose friends carefully.

God will give you the desires of your heart!

Be interested in godly things...and God will fulfill your needs!

Whatever state you're in, be content!

We sometimes stick our heads in the sand, not wanting to see the outside world as it really is.

I would have never met my most valuable friend, the wonderful old grandma, if I had been attached.

When you give God your best, He will bless you with His best.

I determined in my heart, with or without a husband, I want to go to heaven!

Never leave the basics!

15

Views From The Pews
(notes from my scrapbook)

Serve your dad's God wholeheartedly and willingly (I Chronicles 28:9) for the Lord searches all hearts and understands your thoughts.

If you seek Him, He will be found;
If you leave Him, He will reject you.

Keep your attitude sweet and humble and communication will be no problem.

I know why God is God, and not me. I remember getting so tired of praying with young people only to have to pray with them again next

Sunday because they had already backslid. Pretty soon I had no burden to pray.

Instead of responding to the grace of God and allowing it to keep my mind transformed, and the wounds of my relationships healed, I reacted according to human nature and permitted resentment to form.

Family is very permanent in your life. Saints come and go, but your family is always there. I suppose, though, that there are pros and cons with everything, even being a preacher's kid:

Advantages
1. Good moral standards in the home
2. Good friends
3. Respected
4. Leaders of a group
5. Upper middle class society
6. Close family (most of the time)
7. Travel and campmeetings
8. Daughters have more suitors
9. Real parents who know that you are subject to temptation

Disadvantages

1. A lot is expected from you.
2. Being in spotlight (your bad is noticed more than your good).
3. Communication breakdown and fear of condemnation from parents

It is obvious that there are more advantages than disadvantages.

Some of our training in the parsonage was being able to carry on a conversation with non-essential chatter.

I would rather be here with severe trials than pass over the line of never coming back.

16

Jesus, not Denise, Died for Me!

"Deanna, line one please," my secretary called over the intercom.

I picked up the receiver and said, "This is Deanna."

"Hi, watchew' doin'?" came this cheery voice of my sister over the telephone.

"Oh, working," I sighed. "Whatchew' doin'?"

"I just had a minute and wanted to call and tell you I love you," she answered.

"Thanks, you made my day. I love you, too," I replied.

"Well, gotta run. Call me later," she said. "Bye."

"Okay, bye." I placed the receiver into the cradle slowly. She always knows the right time to call, I thought. How neat it is to have a twin.

Several days passed and I had just finished work on Friday, March 13, 1981. I was finishing up the last bit of business when the telephone rang. My boss answered the phone. It was 5:30 p.m. and I was in the door to leave when he said, "Deanna, it's for you. Do you want to take it?"

"Sure, it may be some powerful date," I kidded. "This is Deanna," I answered.

"Deanna," I heard my cousin say on the phone, "Denise and Justin have been in a bad car accident."

"Are they hurt bad? What hospital? Where are they?" I asked. "They are not," she replied quietly. "They are dead."

"They are dead!?" I asked as my body wilted into the chair behind the desk.

My boss came and took the receiver out of my hand and talked to my cousin while I just stared into space. "No, not Denise and Justin, I just talked to her the other day." I kept mumbling as my boss drove me to Denise and Rex's house.

I still couldn't believe it.

When we arrived, the house was filled with Pentecostals. They were everywhere. It seemed like they were just staring. I didn't like any of them.

"Can't a family mourn without you watching to see how long they can take it before they break?" I asked silently.

Mama and Daddy got there and I was

beginning to feel smothered. I wanted to go home for the night but Mama and Daddy kept reminding me, "Honey, you're the only little girl we have now."

Finally, all the people left and it was just us. I asked Mama, "Are all these people this cruel to sit and watch every single tear you cry? I can't handle it." Mama held me close and said softly, "This is our family. Without God and these friends, we couldn't make it. We are drawing our strength from each one of them."

The time came to go to the funeral home. I didn't know which would be worse—the uncertainty of not knowing for sure she and Justin were dead, or to see them lying there. (They had been killed in a fiery auto collision.)

I was having a hard time accepting it when some dear sister came up—and she probably meant well—but it made my emotions boil. She patted me on the back and said, "I heard your sister in the prayer room the other night, and she was praying for God to take her life if it would mean you being saved."

I wheeled around and looked her straight in the eyes and said, "God did not take her because of me. My sister did not serve that kind of a God!"

When I got home, I dug out my Bible from the bottom of a box, and read Isaiah 57:1:

The righteous perisheth, and no man layeth it to heart: and merciful men are taken away, none considering that the righteous is taken away from the evil to come.

I didn't understand, nor do I now understand, why God chose to take Denise and Justin. But this scripture did help my feelings in knowing it wasn't because of me she died.

Jesus, not Denise, died for me!

17

Encounter with God's Love

It was a beautiful sunny Saturday morning. I had slept unusually late. Hoping I could make it to the bank before it closed at noon, I jumped up, slipped on my clothes and left. Now, here I sat on the curb, watching them tow my Mercedes-Benz away. The lady who was in the car that I hit was being wheeled away to the ambulance on a stretcher.

I called a friend who agreed to come pick me up. Tears weren't very far away when his car pulled up and I slid into the passenger seat. I whispered, "Thanks for coming after me."

"Deanna, I knew this was going to happen," he said without raising his voice. "You have got to do something about the way you're living or you won't be alive long. You and I both know your parents couldn't cope with losing another daughter."

He had such a way of bringing me to my senses without getting demonstrative. I knew he was right. He continued with his fatherly advice as we drove to my condominium.

He dropped me off and said he would keep in touch. This was a new lesson I had to learn on my own. I felt so alone as he drove away.

I called Daddy and he suggested I call an acquaintance of his who was a Mercedes-Benz representative. I needed an authoritative person to tell me what to do with the car. Maybe he would take a look at it as a favor to Daddy. I had heard Daddy, Mama, and Rex, my brother in-law, speak very highly of him. I called, only to find he was out of town and would return in a couple of days.

Several days passed and I knew I had to make some decision on my car. Do I have it fixed or sell it wrecked? During this time, I had learned I had no insurance on my car, and with no money to have it repaired, it was a larger problem than I could handle. After paying the medical bills on the lady I hit, my savings were depleted.

The following Tuesday, I decided I had no choice but to try again to get in touch with daddy's friend. I slowly dialed the telephone number, not sure that I really wanted to call.

"Hello," a man's gruff voice answered. Taken aback by the cold, unfriendly voice, I softly asked for the man by name.

"Speaking," he said, in the same gruff voice. For a few seconds I had my doubts whether this was too smart of a call. This man sounds as if he could bite my head off. It's too late now, I thought as I blundered on.

"This is Deanna Neely, and Daddy suggested I call you. I have had a wreck and since you know about Mercedes, I need your expertise and advice."

Whew! I must have sounded friendly because his voice seemed to relax as he told me where he had been when I called earlier. We arranged to meet so he could look at my car. In the process of all of this, he shared with me what all God had done for him. Our backgrounds ran so parallel, and the coincidence of him having a twin brother made it easy for me to talk freely about my feelings in losing my twin sister.

After I had shown him my wrecked car, he took me back to work and for the first time in my life I heard the words, "God loves you." I smiled and thanked him for his kindness, but quickly discovered that he had something else to say. He brought out this small Bible from his pocket and began to read some scriptures—"Sins as far as East from West...Sea of forgetfulness...Faithful to forgive." Tears welled up in my eyes as I looked at him and said, "I don't think God can forgive me. I've been too bad and done too many things wrong." He assured me that God was real big and would have no memory of those things if I would just ask Him to forgive me.

I opened the car door and muttered that I had to get back to work. I really wanted to get out of his car because I was feeling God's love as he spoke, and I must be strong and not start crying. I'm sure somewhere in my life, I had heard God could forgive or we wouldn't have had new people in our church finding God. But I had never listened.

I tried to forget this encounter but I kept hearing his words that God could forgive and forget!

> Publisher's Note
>
> This concludes Deanna's hand-written notes. Circumstances later brought her to a place of repentance and the acceptance of God's forgiveness.

18

The Parents' Perspective

by Vernon and Dolores Neely

How devastating and heart-breaking it is for parents to see their child walk away from home, church and the Lord to seek the pleasures of the world. It is like a bad dream. This is not supposed to happen to us. A parent goes through a lot of agonizing self-appraisal: "Oh, what did I do wrong to cause our child to make such a choice? Maybe I was too strict, or maybe I wasn't sensitive enough to her needs and feelings. Maybe I did not spend enough time with her. I feel I have been a complete failure as a parent." The list goes on and on to blame ourselves for our child's choices and actions. In retrospect, some of these things could be true.

When I go back to the Bible and review the story of the prodigal son, there is no indication that his decision to take his inheritance early and go into a far country was that his father was not a decent, good, and understanding person. It does not say that his life at home was so miserable because his parents were too strict, abusive, or over-bearing. Just the opposite was true. When he asked for his inheritance his father complied without hesitation. His father was not faulted in the story told by Jesus.

The truth of the matter was that he had made his mind up that he wanted to try his wings and go his way. The same is true with many of our children today. They just exercise their God-given right to choose. There is no reason for them to blame their parents or anyone else for their choices. They may try to excuse themselves by pointing a finger, but that is not a new thing. It's as old as mankind. When God asked Adam if he had eaten of the forbidden tree, he said, "This woman whom thou gavest to be with me, she gave me of the tree, and I did eat." And then the Lord God said unto the woman, "What is this that thou hast done?"

And the woman said, "The serpent beguiled me, and I did eat."

Many can be our excuses, but the truth is that we make our own choices. Like Adam and Eve, we must live with the consequences of those choices.

I am sure I could have been a better Dad in many ways. Even though our daughter chose to leave the church and ultimately the family, I am not guilt-ridden. I feel that her mother and I did the best we knew to do at the time.

I have no regrets for having held to Bible principles and teachings with our children. By holding to these principles, all three of our children believed and held to them—even Deanna, the prodigal. The Bible says in Proverbs 22:6, "Train up a child in the way he should go; and when he is old, he will not depart from it."

In July 1999, Deanna was diagnosed with Acute Myaloid Lukemia. This was a terrible ordeal for her and also for her mother and me. We totally gave our time and attention to her during her illness. She saw and felt our love. She wanted us close and we willingly complied. We took up residence in a house across the street from Brigham and Women's Hospital in Boston so we could take turns at her bedside.

One day when she was very sick I was standing at her bedside talking to her. She looked up at me and asked, "Daddy (she was my little blonde-headed girl even though she was forty-six years old), do you think I am going to make it?"

I was having a struggle with this same question, but after a moment of consideration I said, "Yes, baby, I believe you will make it." (She did for almost a year.) She then said, "Daddy read to me out of my Bible." When I opened her Bible I saw it was marked and high-lighted throughout, especially in the Psalms. I read to her. Then she whispered, "Daddy, sing a song to me." Immediately the chorus of an old familiar song came to me and I began to sing:

Jesus, Jesus, You know what's best for me.
Lead on, Jesus, I'll go wherever You lead.

We both wept.

Deanna went through a bone marrow transplant on November 24, 1999. The donor was her own brother, Michael. His marrow was a perfect match to hers and for a little over a year it gave her life. She suffered severe ups and downs during this year, even to being paralyzed from her waist down.

Deanna's husband, Jim Merchant, was very faithful during this time to be with her and provide loving comfort. He was a great help to her and to us. He took off work many days to be with her and to assist us. His sincere loyalty at such a time was deeply appreciated by Deanna and our entire family.

In spite of all her suffering, we still were concerned that Deanna had not completely fallen upon the stone, Christ Jesus, to be broken. Then just before Thanksgiving, 2000, I was praying in our home and asked the Lord to restore Deanna to complete wholeness. The Lord spoke to me through a very strong impression that there were thousands of people praying for Deanna and that He could heal her, but Deanna was going to have to touch Him for herself—like the woman in the Bible with the issue of blood. She was going to have to press through the crowd of doubt, fear, resentment, and rebellion to touch the Lord for herself and she could be made whole. I felt I had to convey this to Deanna. I told my wife I had to do this whether she understood or not.

We went to be at her bedside in Boston around Thanksgiving. I told her that I had something to talk to her about so her mother, hearing this, stepped out of the room so we could be alone. I began to tell her of my prayer and the Lord's revelation to me about what she must do. She listened intently and when I had finished we both were crying. I held her close and felt no resentment from her. She seemed totally submitted to the Lord. I felt that the prodigal had come home and both Fathers—her heavenly Father and her earthly Father—welcomed her home.

Moms and dads, don't give up on your prodigal. Your story can have a happy ending, too.

Note: Deanna went home to her heavenly Father on December 14, 2000.

Through a mother's eyes:

One never thinks of what it will take to raise a child when the maternal bug bites. To have and to hold a precious, lovable baby is all the mind can think upon. To a young woman desiring a baby, it never enters into our thoughts to ask the question, "Will my child have complexities and problems that I, as its mother, will not know how to handle?"

No one on earth does all things perfectly. Given the situations and circumstances of life, they do what they feel is right at the time.

When I looked into a baby crib and saw two little girls that were mine, I began to realize the weight of two tiny souls. I prayed for the Lord to help me raise them.

Through the years I tried to be fair in every way when dealing with the girls, but I learned that "being fair" was not enough, for they were not alike. One was ready to meet the world with what she believed and stood for while the other one met it with a shy smile and downcast eyes.

Deanna was about twelve years old when she came into the kitchen one evening when I was preparing our evening meal. When I looked at her I knew she was troubled about something and I asked what was bothering her. She looked at me with tears coming to her eyes and said, "Mama, everybody thinks Denise is pretty and I am ugly."

I immediately told her she was as pretty as her sister, but she didn't want to hear that from me because she already knew what I thought. (Right about that time I was mighty unhappy with some gossips that did not notice an innocent little girl listening to their conversation.)

"Deanna," I said, "you know there are some pretty little girls that are not pretty on the inside, and the inside is what counts. The most important thing is to have Jesus inside you. He makes you pretty. If you would like to be different, start working on your personality."

She didn't say very much after our talk, but I noticed her not being as shy and talking with people more. Evidently she asked the Lord to help her for He did.

When problems came my way I always felt if I could go pray through the situation that had arisen, I would make it to the next trial. I thought I had taught my children this solution. Sometimes it is easier to take matters into our own hands than "go pray through."

At our house there never was a choice of staying home or going to church, we just knew when church time came around we would be going to the house of God. Yes, that was training. Like having family prayer together every night. We all knew that God was the core and focal point of our lives. This is an anchor to a child.

Who can say what happens inside a person,

young or old, when they decide to turn from Jesus. It is truly hard to accept, but accept it we must, for we can only make choices for ourselves and not for others.

There was a day Deanna and I had to come to a truce. She would pick and goad me so much that I thought she hated me when I was around her longer than a day. I finally I told her, "You accept me the way I am and I will accept you the way you are and maybe we can get along. Just remember one thing, Deanna, I am not going to change the way I live for God." Looking back I think she wanted me to say just those words. Her Daddy, brother, sister and I were a lighthouse for her in the midst of her worldly storm.

At the airport where Deanna worked, she was wheeling a man down an incline to the airplane when the wheelchair got away from her and the man fell to the floor. Deanna began to loudly pray, "Jesus! God help me!!" When she told me this it made me know that in a crisis the first thing she would do is pray and ask the Lord to help her no matter who was around.

In the many weeks and months of Deanna's illness, I came to the assurance she loved me. She wanted me with her. Late one night at the Brigham and Women's Hospital in Boston, Deanna looked at me and said, "Mama, I wish God would just take me on."

I leaned over her bed and asked, "Deanna, are you ready to go on?"

She said, "Yes, ma'am, I am."

She knew what I was asking her and she assured me she had made everything all right with her heavenly Father and was ready to go to His home.

Deanna never really got over the death of her twin sister, Denise, and her nephew, Justin. She told me that there were times when she would think and act just like Denise. There are still mysteries about twins. There was not a day that Denise did not pray for her sister to be saved. Those tears were bottled up in heaven, and who knows whose tears got through to the throne of

God.

It has been said, "There is safety in a strong father." That has been proven true in our household. I thank God for my husband's faithful stand for truth and his uncompromising, yet compassionate way he managed the affairs of our family and our homelife.

Even in the worse times when our prodigal walked on our hearts with cleats on her shoes, she was still my child and I loved her. God never gave me any throwaways. Children can never know the heartache and sadness they can cause a parent until they become one. Even then they may choose to live in a fantasy world or rush toward destruction with the enemy of their soul screaming, "That's the way to go!"

Some children are easy to correct and then there are others you have to follow to the rim of hell—never giving them up. When they do turn from being a prodigal, we have all won.

My mother once told me, "Honey, raising children is a knee route." What she was telling me is when raising children you have to pray a whole lot. Raising my children has been just that—taking them to the Lord every day. When my grandchildren were born they were added one by one to that list and now my great grandchildren. They are never too young for a mother or grandmother to pray for their mate in life, and for the protecting power of God daily. To all my children I say, "Don't expect me to change."

19

A Brother's Viewpoint

"If you want to see Deanna again you need to get here as soon as you can."

Within hours of receiving that message, my wife Cheri and I were sitting on the American Airlines flight from Houston to Boston attempting to absorb the shocking news—shocking because just a couple of days earlier Deanna was excitedly discussing with me her plans for coming home to Texas for Christmas. Now it all seemed like a dream. Could she really be that bad? Did she in fact have only hours to live? What caused the turn for the worse? There were so many questions with very few answers. We remembered how, to the amazement of the doctors, the Lord had raised her up from certain death just months before. Now we were facing this grave news. As we drew closer to Boston, we wanted to have faith—but why was the family contemplating removing the life supports?

Our drive from the airport to the Brigham and Women's/Dana Farber Cancer Hospital was reminiscent of the previous year, when on Thanksgiving eve just one year ago we were filled with hope and expectation, preparing for the bone marrow transplant for which I was the donor. Everything went well with the transplant from the start—a perfect match of our bone marrow types to the immediate improvement in her leukemia. Now we were rushing through those same corridors, but this time with feelings of apprehension and fear.

Mother met us in the hall leading into the intensive care unit and gently warned us that we may not recognize Deanna since her kidneys were not functioning well and she had some swelling. As I looked down at the form lying on the bed I could hardly believe it was my sister. The pneumonia was taking it's toll causing fluid retention and extreme swelling. A breathing tube was taped to the side of her face. The sight was quite disturbing. This couldn't be Deanna, she is only forty-six and this looked like a very sick elderly woman. We just weren't prepared for this. As the doctors had instructed, we talked to Deanna as if she were awake, speaking positively, expressing our love to her. Our family prayed around her bedside trusting the will of the Lord to be done. She passed away shortly thereafter on December 14, 2000.

The memorial service in Fairhaven, Massachusetts was very comforting and sweet. Deanna would have been happy. I was amazed that in just a short time she had cultivated so many friendships and had made such an impact on her husband Jim's family. His cousins and family members were broken-hearted. I saw a stoic old fisherman wipe tears from his eyes unashamedly. Sorrow was evidenced on the faces of her business associates from American Airlines and from her real estate office, which spoke volumes to me. Pastor Nathan Scoggins delivered a beautiful message on "The Mark Of A Godly Heritage." The service was something many of those in attendance had never experienced. They came expecting a mass but instead were involved in a moving Pentecostal service. Brother Scoggins made a striking analogy of the quilt Deanna kept on her bed for comfort throughout her entire hospitalization, made by our ninety-three year old grandmother, Grace Neely. He spoke of her being "covered by the quilt Grace made," but ultimately Deanna was covered by another quilt of grace— God's grace.

On the flight to Dallas for the funeral we talked about everything that had happened and about the times we had spent with Deanna and Jim during the years she had lived in Massachusetts. She was always so excited when we came to stay a few days. She would arrange to be off work, spending the entire time taking us from place to place. After a few of our excursions throughout the Cape Cod area, it became easy to see why she had fallen in love with this beautiful and historical part of America. We recalled how Deanna had maintained her strong Texas accent and used it to her benefit. Everyone loved it, and no one could keep from smiling when they would hear that Texas drawl.

Tears and smiles alternated during our flight as we thought about the different aspects of Deanna's life. It seems that when a loved one is taken in death the insignificant things become important, because memories are all that remain of that person. Cheri recalled that she and Deanna had agreed that they were "real" sisters—none of this sister-in-law stuff for them. Cheri and I we were both very sad for our loss.

When we were young, Deanna was always the one with the good sense of humor. She could seemingly make something funny out of the most serious of situations. She was mild and generally kind with her practical jokes, however. I recalled the time I sat on the porch swing with a girlfriend—feeling so grown up—and Deanna serenaded us with the song "Blue, Blue, My World Is Blue." I later found out that she chose this song because she did not like that girl very much, especially as a choice for her brother.

Deanna always made holidays a special

time. We were always so excited before Christmas when we would find gifts we knew Deanna would "just love."

In Little Bethel Cemetery in Duncanville, TX, Deanna was buried just on the other side of a big elm tree from Denise. This was something that was hard to grasp—both of my sisters were gone. I stood and stared at the grave marker: "Denise Elaine Johnson August 7, 1954 to March 13, 1981," and "Justin Dale Johnson February 13, 1977 to March 13, 1981." It seemed like such a short time since we had been at this cemetery burying them, but it had been almost twenty years. Deanna had wanted to be buried beside Denise, and our brother-in-law, Rex, had generously agreed that this was how it should be. After a few comforting words by the ministers and friends, we left the cold, windy cemetery and it was all over.

The following week was Christmas and we were all gathered as usual at Daddy and Mother's home in Lufkin. Aunt Mollie was there, and we were happy that Jim could also be with us. We visited and talked of Deanna and how much we missed her, thanking the Lord that she was ready to meet Him. We took comfort in knowing that she was now in a wonderful place. Little Isaac Neely, our new grandson, took our minds back to the excitement of Christmas. After all the gift opening, trying on clothes, and oohing and ahhing over everyone gifts, we were talking and someone mentioned a book Deanna had begun to write. The next day the manuscript was circulated around, and after reading it we all felt that it was something others might find helpful and encouraging.

Her musings took me back to the time we were kids and teenagers. There were references to events I remembered happening and conversations I remembered having, but in a way it was somewhat of an eye opener as to Deanna's perspective on our childhood. She mentioned events that in my memory were insignificant, but that is the difference in people—even among children raised in the same home.

We were reared by loving, God-fearing parents who felt that it was of utmost importance that our entire family lived the beliefs taught by our dad and the church. The expectations were high, but there was so much love in our home that it was a joy to be obedient. The sixties were a time of social turmoil and the church wanted to insure none of its young people would be caught up in the wave of rebellion sweeping the country. Their well-meaning admonitions may have seemed over-bearing, evoking resentment among some of the youth of the Pentecostal faith. These were the days of the "fellowship meetings," which seemed to serve as a forum for ministers to impress the others with just how strict their teachings were.

I am so thankful that I remained faithful to the Lord until the day I realized that He actually loved me and wanted me to be saved even more than I wanted to be saved. What a difference that realization made in the happiness I have found in serving God. The joy in serving the Lord is such a wonderful thing, but I feel sad for those who left the church before they were able to realize the love of God.

Talks that Deanna and I had many years ago on the topic of the mistakes we make in our lives revealed some of the erroneous beliefs she held regarding sin and condemnation. The message emanating from the church often became lost when perceived as a burden of rules rather than a system of morals. One can obey rules without having a clear understanding of the importance of being a person of high moral character. When we reduce our core beliefs to a list of "don'ts," our character is weakened.

Deanna said to me on a couple of occasions, "If I think it, I might as well do it." It was a mistaken notion, but she felt that if so much as one rule was broken she might as well throw in the towel since she was going to hell anyway. She was so much like other prodigals who didn't feel that there was room to be human and still obtain God's forgiveness. The problem with taking those critical steps away from the church is that they will always take us farther than we plan to go.

I have often felt that our perspective governs our happiness. At one place in her writings

Deanna related a story of our family's move from Abilene to Odessa and how she was the one given the uncomfortable room with the five doors. I believe that this is a prime example of how the devil can influence our minds to feel that a short period of inconvenience, or even being done wrong, can be escalated into a giant incident which justifies our right to feel persecuted. What was missing from the story was when we moved into the new parsonage approximately six months later, for her previous sacrifice, Deanna got to choose any room she wanted. She had the largest bedroom in the house, right next to the bathroom, and included was a new canopy bedroom suite. Denise got a very small room with the old fifties vintage bedroom suite purchased by our parents shortly after they were married. I never heard Denise complain. For Deanna, the negative experience was a memory that had made a lasting impression—not the positive blessing that came later. A wrong frame of mind can skew the self-image of the prodigal and create resentment for the sacrifices in lifestyle which are expected of us to be pleasing to the Lord.

At times I felt sorry for Deanna as she struggled with living the biblical standards. So seldom were the times that she gladly wore the longer skirt or willingly left off the make-up. Inwardly she desired to do the right thing and live a pleasing life before the Lord, but peer pressure and her desire for acceptance would invariably drag her down into a state of discouragement. I couldn't always sympathize with her since I had resolved in my mind to serve the Lord—although I often worried that God may be looking for a chance to zap me the moment I erred. To me, it was still worth it to be faithful. I also remember those times of spiritual refreshing when Deanna would be so blessed and cleansed by tears during those wonderful altar services. We felt so close during those times and we all shared a common commitment to the church.

Deanna married shortly after I did and her first husband was a good friend of mine. He had come into the church about a year before they married. He was a new convert and was really on fire, serving the Lord with fervor. They loved to sing together and even sang with Denise in a trio while he played his guitar. For a while they seemed to be happy, but they began to feel that just a little slipping here and there would not hurt their walk with God. He was an example of someone who wasn't able to just dabble with sin. He had lived a life of sin before coming to the Lord and he began leading Deanna down a road she really didn't intend to take. Sadly the marriage reached a state where there was no room for recovery. As she relates in her story, her trip took her to the bottom where she was forced to make some important choices and critical changes.

During the years that Deanna was away from God, our relationship was strained. We wanted to enjoy our times together but it was difficult since we were so far apart spiritually. We wanted to talk about the church and all that was happening but she was just not interested in "church" things. Sometimes we would catch up on everything that had been happening to the friends from our teenage years. We would tell her of those who had asked about her, passing messages along from those who had been her close friends during her earlier years.

Coupled with the terrible tragedy that claimed the life of our precious sister Denise, Deanna's backsliding was somewhat like losing both sisters. Virtually all of the things we had in common were lost. I have often felt that wayward ones never realize the effect of their choices on other members of the family.

I believe down deep Deanna really loved the Lord and wanted to do the right thing, but circumstances and the cares of life kept her from what she really desired to do. After reaching the bottom, she made a turn in her life and began to live a more upstanding life. In her heart she knew that the day would come when she would have to make that commitment to go all the way with God before she would really be happy. She may have resented it at times, but I believe she was comforted by the fact that she knew Mother and Daddy were always praying for her. I'm sure the combined prayers for God to "save Deanna" number into the hundreds or thousands.

During the last summer, Deanna was in the hospital sick with some sort of spinal disease, and mother began to talk to her about her condition with the Lord. They prayed together and Mother expressed encouragement that God was going to do something for Deanna. It was soon after that that the Lord raised her up. The doctors could only explain it as a miracle. We were rejoicing in the hope that this had begun the healing that would bring her back to both physical and spiritual wholeness. I believe the Lord often will work miracles like this to let us know He is able to heal, even if later He chooses not to heal another disorder that eventually claims the life.

Just before Thanksgiving 2000, the Lord impressed Dad that he should tell Deanna the story from the Bible of the woman with the issue of blood—the main point being that she had to touch the Lord for herself. Unlike the times before when Dad would be met with resistance, she responded with weeping and a prayer of praise and commitment to God. Dad told us of the wonderful time of refreshing they had together, and the peace and comfort they felt. How timely, for in less than three weeks she was gone.

I was sitting in service on Sunday morning after we had returned to Houston and Pastor Kilgore asked for those who had a need for healing, finances, etc., to lift their hand. Then, as his custom often is, he said, "If you want prayer for the salvation of a loved one lift the other hand." It suddenly dawned on me—every time I had lifted my hand for Deanna it had been seen by the Lord, and he had not failed to answer my prayer.

Mike

Deanna's Song

The words and melody of the song below were written by Deanna in 1972 when she was 17 years old. She sung it in church a number of times. Her brother-in-law, Rex Johnson (whom she affectionately called "Rexie Dale") sung it at her funeral.

Waters That's All Passed Away

Trials came that I thought
    would never leave,
And there were mountains
    that seemed so steep;
But the goodness of the Lord
    removed them all
When at the altar I had to finally fall.

Now I thank God it's as waters
    that's all passed away,
And there's a peace that suddenly came.
There's not a reason to ever doubt
    the Lord again,
'Cause it's as waters that's all passed away.